**W9-AYO-206**

## DATE DUE

| | | | |
|---|---|---|---|
| | | | |
| | | | |
| | | | |
| | | | |
| | | | |
| | | | |
| | | | |
| | | | |
| | | | |
| | | | |
| | | | |
| | | | |
| | | | |
| | | | |
| | | | |
| | | | |
| | | | |
| | | | |

THE HISPANIC INFLUENCE IN THE UNITED STATES

# LATINOS
## IN AMERICAN HISTORY

# ANTONIO LOPEZ DE SANTA ANNA

BY JOHN BANKSTON

*Mitchell Lane*
**PUBLISHERS**

P.O. Box 196
Hockessin, Delaware 19707

# OTHER TITLES IN THE SERIES

Visit us on the web: www.mitchelllane.com
Comments? email us: mitchelllane@mitchelllane.com

THE HISPANIC INFLUENCE IN THE UNITED STATES

# LATINOS
## IN AMERICAN HISTORY

# ANTONIO LOPEZ DE
# SANTA ANNA

BY JOHN BANKSTON

Printing  1        2        3        4        5        6        7        8        9

Library of Congress Cataloging-in-Publication Data

Bankston, John, 1974-
     Antonio López de Santa Anna / by John Bankston.
        p. cm. — (Latinos in American history)
Includes bibliographical references and index.
     ISBN 1-58415-209-5 (Library Bound)
    1. Santa Anna, Antonio López de, 1794?-1876—Juvenile literature. 2. Mexico—History—1821-1861—Juvenile literature. 3. Texas—History—To 1846—Juvenile literature. 4. Presidents—Mexico—Biography—Juvenile literature. 5. Generals—Mexico—Biography—Juvenile literature. I. Title. II. Series.
     F1232.S232B36 2003
     972'.04'092--dc21
                              2003000352

ABOUT THE AUTHOR:  Born in Boston, Massachusetts, John Bankston has written over three dozen biographies for young adults profiling scientists like Jonas Salk and Alexander Fleming, celebrities like Mandy Moore and Alicia Keys, great achievers like Alfred Nobel, and master musicians like Franz Peter Schubert. He has worked in Los Angeles, California as a producer, screenwriter and actor. Currently he is in pre-production on *Dancing at the Edge*, a semi-autobiographical film he hopes to film in Portland, Oregon.  Last year he completed his first young adult novel, *18 to Look Younger*.

PHOTO CREDITS: Cover: Texas State Library & Archives Commission; p. 6 Texas State Library & Archives Commission; p. 9 Hulton/Archive; p. 10 Texas State Library & Archives Commission; p. 13 Charles & Josette Lenars/Corbis; p. 16 Bettmann/Corbis; p. 20 Texas State Library & Archives Commission; p. 22 Corbis; p. 25 Bob Krist/Corbis; p.28 Bettmann/Corbis; p. 30 SuperStock; p. 32 Bettmann/Corbis; p. 34 Hulton/Archive; p. 37 Hulton/Archive; p. 39 Texas State Library & Archives Commission; p. 40 Bettmann/Corbis

PUBLISHER'S NOTE: This story is based on the author's extensive research, which he believes to be accurate.

    The spelling of the names in this book follow the generally accepted usage of modern day. The spelling of Spanish names in English has evolved over time with no consistency. Many names have been anglicized and no longer use the accent marks or any Spanish grammar. Others have retained the Spanish grammar. Hence, we refer to Hernando de Soto as "de Soto," but Francisco Vásquez de Coronado as "Coronado." There are other variances as well. Some sources might spell Vásquez as Vazquez. For the most part, we have adapted the more widely recognized spellings.

# CONTENTS

*Davy Crockett was a famous frontiersman who died in battle at the Alamo in 1836. His death, along with 180 others outraged many in the United States.*

# REMEMBER THE ALAMO!

T he Mexican Army hit the villages first. Cutting through many of the country's provinces on their way to fight the rebels in Texas, the military raided the small towns. Teenage boys and young men were taken at gunpoint. They became conscripts—soldiers against their will.

Their only other choice was death.

Trailing the men were their mothers and wives, brothers and sisters. Children barely old enough to walk marched beside old people—entire families followed the Army.

Many were Indios—native Americans who were unprepared for the long march north. Most were barefoot, while the luckier ones wore sandals. The women and children foraged for food—the Mexican Army didn't have enough money to feed them.

But the villagers weren't enough. The army needed even more men. So the jails were emptied, murderers and thieves pressed into service.

The conscripts were given some brief military training, out-of-date muskets and the uniforms of men who'd died before them. The ones who tried to desert were shot.

They looked like an unruly mob, not a professional army. Only the officers with their crisp uniforms and expensive weapons looked like professional soldiers. The conscripts formed the front line: poorly trained, badly equipped and easily replaced.

There were thousands of them as they moved towards Texas and the Alamo. Once a mission in San Antonio de Béxar where Spanish priests converted native tribes to the Christian religion, it now served as a fort for a handful of rebellious American citizens called "Texicans." They had come to Texas for a new life and new opportunities. Instead they'd balked at the Mexican government's harsh laws. The Alamo would become their last stand.

But before the Mexican Army could face the Texicans, they had to face the weather. Led by a man who called himself "The Napoleon of the West," they were about to run into the type of weather which helped defeat the original Napoleon. As the ill-prepared army marched north towards Texas, they encountered a "blue norther." This was a sudden drop in temperature, where wind and snow blasted officer and conscript alike. Most of the Indios had never seen snow before. They didn't know how to handle freezing temperatures. Hundreds died, buried beneath a burial shroud of white powder. The children and the elderly fared the worst.

Even daylight didn't bring relief. Just as they were recovering from the night's storm, the Commences attacked. The Commences were the fiercest of the native tribes—more warlike even than the Apaches, they went after the unprotected positions, killing quickly and then disappearing.

Despite the losses, the Mexican Army marched on. They reached the Alamo in late February of 1836. Inside its walls about 180 rebels defended their position. They included Davy Crockett, the Tennessee frontiersman whose exploits were immortalized in song, and Jim Bowie, with the knife he made famous.

The battle lasted for thirteen days. It ended in the early morning hours on March 6 with a final successful rush of conscripts breaking through the walls. Though hundreds of Mexicans were killed, their vastly superior numbers turned the tide. The bloodshed was rapid. The few Texicans who weren't killed in the battle were quickly executed. The dead weren't buried. Instead the corpses were burned. It took two full days for the fire to consume them all.

The executions and cremations were against the code that most battles are fought under. This harsh treatment was one reason that the cry of "Remember the Alamo!" inspired so many to fight against Mexico's power.

While their rage was directed at an entire country, one man was responsible for the executions, the burning, and many of the other harsh things done in Mexico's name. He grew up in a society where his birthplace normally would have meant he would never know power. Instead he became both president and emperor of his country. But although he became wealthy and famous, he died in poverty and obscurity.

His name is Antonio López de Santa Anna. Many called him the Eagle. The nickname came from an Aztec legend about an eagle leading the way to a promised city. An eagle decorated the Mexican flag after the country won its independence from Spain.

Antonio Santa Anna is as much a part of Mexican legend as the eagle myth. He is also as much a part of American history as the Alamo. He could be brutal, cunning and immoral. In his lifetime he altered the borders of two countries.■

*Although they were outnumbered, the defenders of the Alamo held the fort for nearly two weeks. Davy Crockett, shown here with a rifle held over his head, died in the final siege. "Remember the Alamo" would become a rallying cry for Texas independence.*

*Antonio Lopez de Santa Anna grew up in a time when someone born in Mexico couldn't be president. Despite being born in Mexico, in his lifetime he would become president, general and even a dictator.*

# AMBITION

I t could be a small European country or right here in the United States. Every time voters drop a ballot in a ballot box, they're participating in a process that was unimaginable just a few hundred years ago. Until fairly recent times, most countries didn't hold elections. Decisions weren't made by senators, presidents or prime ministers. They were made by kings and queens, emperors and empresses. Members of royal families gained their power by birth, not elections. Their country's citizens had little power.

The royals' control extended to the New World. As land seized by exploration in North America gave way to established settlements, Britain ruled the eastern colonies, French properties ran along the middle of the continent and Spanish territories covered the south and the west. Regardless of the "mother country," all of these colonists were "royal subjects."

They too were powerless.

In the late eighteenth century, things began to change.

Beginning in the 1770s, British colonists rebelled. What started out as a few isolated incidents led to the American Revolution, the Declaration of Independence and eventually the system of government we enjoy today. The colonists' victory inspired other rebellions. In France, the middle classes and the peasants surged against the notorious Bastille prison on July 14, 1789. They unseated their rulers and marched hundreds to their death at the infamous guillotine. The bloodshed repulsed many, but it led to changes in numerous govern- ments across Europe. Kings and queens slowly relinquished some of their power.

Other revolutions were brewing.

The Spanish were tolerant rulers. Liberal reforms in Spain hap- pened long before the revolutions in France and the United States. Spanish citizens enjoyed freedoms unheard of in most monarchies. Yet in Mexico, Spanish power was as strong and controlling as ever. By the 1790s, some Mexicans began to dream of living in a free and separate country. Their attempts to gain independence were brutally crushed.

In the New World, Spanish territories stretched from California across the Southwest to the region which would become Texas. In all of North America, there was not a city as populous as Mexico City, and few regions were as settled as the area south of the Rio Grande River. Missions and settlements in Mexico predated those in the more north- ern colonies by well over a century.

Another important city was Veracruz. Located on the Gulf of Mexico, it was Mexico's largest port. Taxes and fees collected from ships arriving and departing helped keep the Spanish treasury filled. While the Spanish military wasn't what it once had been, it was still strong enough to keep the natives and colonists under submission.

In Veracruz, Spanish power was a harsh reality. Warships lying in the harbor provided the citizens with a daily reminder of Spanish naval strength. If that wasn't intimidating enough, in the entire city no building was as large or as imposing as the San Juan de Ulúa prison. The facility, which covered a small island just off the coast, was consid- ered by many to be the cruelest prison on the planet. Many of its prisoners became revolutionaries upon their release.

From tiny homes to enormous cathedrals, Veracruz gleamed like a polished smile as building after building featured brilliant white paint. It was a place overflowing with style, commerce, and opportunity.

It was also a place overflowing with disease.

In the hot and humid summer months, plagues swept through the area. Yellow fever took its deadly toll throughout the entire year. Yet

*Surrounded by a moat, the fearsome Castillo de Juan Ulúa prison was the most visible landmark to visitors. But the residents feared disease more than they feared imprisonment.*

the population continued to swell behind its stately ivory walls. The city's outward appearance contrasted with the horrors of its prison and the thousands dying from sickness.

Veracruz was home to an ambitious businessman named Antonio Lopez de Santa Anna. In addition to business, he'd managed to rise to the low-level post of sub-delegate, but this was as far as he could go. He would never be able to make the decisions and laws which affected his people's lives.

That was because Antonio was a criollo (pronounced cree-OH-low). Criollos were considered "pureblooded." That is, they were Catholics able to trace their families directly to Spain without any Moorish or Jewish blood in their background. Criollos were considered solid members of the middle class. But they were not considered fit to govern. That was because they had been born in Mexico and not in Spain.

Governing was left to the peninsulares, who were not only "pureblooded" but also Spanish born. They took their name from the fact that Spain occupied most of what is called the Iberian Peninsula in Europe. These were the men who made the rules in Mexico. They arrived by ship in Veracruz. Although they usually only stayed for a short period of time, they held all the power. Mexicans resented being ruled by people who weren't connected to their country.

Mexico, like many countries in Europe, was class-oriented. Who your parents were dictated where you went to school, what kind of job you held, even who you married. Although criollos could be very successful, the mestizos, who had a mixture of Spanish and native bloodlines, were usually servants or laborers. The Indios, members of native tribes who'd lived in Mexico hundreds of years before the first Spanish arrived, were considered the lowest class and were also treated the worst.

Eventually this would change. Even Indios would have a chance to make the laws in Mexico.

However, on February 21, 1794, the class system was still the law of the land. On that day, Antonio was traveling northwest to see his wife Manuela. She was in labor at their second home in Jalapa, sixty miles away.

The couple wasn't rich. But for many residents of Veracruz, a second home wasn't a luxury. It was a necessity. Those who couldn't afford to leave often died young because of the unhealthy conditions.

Jalapa was located at the base of the 18,000-foot-high volcano Pico de Orizaba. The town had already given its name to the famous Jalapeño chili pepper. It is also the birthplace of one of the most memorable of all Mexican citizens. For it was here that Antonio and Manuela had a son. His full name was Antonio López de Santa-Anna Pérez de Lebrón.

Shortened to Santa Anna, his name would later become infamous in Texas.

Antonio attended school as a teen, but he couldn't wait to leave. He saw men without education making their fortunes. He listened to the stories of adventure from the sailors and military men who'd come from Cuba and Spain. He heard stories of fighting native tribes and revolutionaries.

By the time he was fourteen, Antonio had left school. He felt that he was ready to make his own way in the world. In spite of his abbreviated education, for the rest of his life Antonio distinguished himself with his excellent command of the Spanish language. He spoke with a slow precision which set him apart from most of his peers.

After he left school, Antonio's father arranged for him to serve an apprenticeship to a wealthy merchant. This means he would work and learn a trade for free. It could have made him rich. But Antonio didn't want a life of buying and selling.

"I have since my earliest years been drawn to the glorious career of arms, feeling it to be my true vocation and calling," he explained in the first chapter of *The Eagle: The Autobiography of Santa Anna*. "On the ninth of July, in the year 1810, with my parents' blessing, I enlisted as a first class cadet in the permanent infantry regiment of Veracruz."

He was sixteen years old, and his dreams of adventure were closer than he knew.■

*Father Miguel Hidalgo was a courageous priest who led the first organized revolt against Spanish rule. His beheading was meant to be a lesson—instead it inspired a revolution.*

# INDEPENDENCE

A t an age when most teens today are dealing with high school, Antonio was dealing with combat against hostile enemies. Because of his middle class background, Antonio Santa Anna was immediately made an officer in the Royal Army of Spain, a pretty heady set of responsibilities for someone as young as he was.

He handled it well.

Still living part-time with his parents, Antonio was given orders to join General Joaquín Arredondo's army in 1811. There was a rebellion in the northern provinces and Antonio would help stop it. The year before, a priest named Miguel Hidalgo wrote a document called "Grito de Dolores" ("Cry of Dolores"). The priest wanted his countrymen to break free from Spain. For many Mexicans, it would be their Declaration of Independence. Hidalgo led 20,000 rebels until his capture. After he was executed by firing squad, his head was cut off and displayed on a pole for the next ten years. Many more of his countrymen followed his lead, and many of them would follow him into death.

Antonio killed more than his fair share of rebels. Over two years of campaigning, his willingness to charge in and fight no matter what the odds or risks led to a promotion from the infantry to the elite cavalry.

He also got his first taste of what it would be like to fight Americans, those who'd lived in the United States and moved south to the province of Texas.

The pioneer Americans in Texas were courageous dreamers. They built ranches and bred cattle, they married local women, they learned to speak Spanish and befriended the local tribes.

What they refused to do was bow down to the Spanish crown. They raised an army, largely financed by the U.S. government. They won several battles against Royalist troops in 1813. Soon they had advanced as far as San Antonio de Béxar.

That brought them to the attention of Arredondo, who crossed the Rio Grande River with a force of just under 2000 men. The two sides met beneath the scorching heat of the August sun. It became a bloodbath later remembered as the Battle of Medina.

The rebel army set up an ambush. But when a scout from Arredondo's army approached, they opened fire on the man. That gave away their positions.

Arredondo was in a secure defensive position. He also had cannons. When the rebels attacked, dozens were cut down when the big guns began firing. Dozens more fell victim to massed volleys from his disciplined troops.

It was a slaughter. Only the Indios were allowed to escape. The Americans and their Mexican allies who survived to retreat were followed on horseback, and shot down like foxes in a hunting party.

The aftermath made the battle seem mild. American and Mexican prisoners were forced to dig trenches. Wooden planks were placed over the pits, and the men were marched over them. There they were shot, pitching head first into their graves.

The victorious Mexicans rode into San Antonio de Béxar. The atrocities continued. Men suspected of supporting the rebels were rounded up. Every day, several were killed, then hacked into pieces. Their families were also punished.

Still a teenager, Antonio received a medal for bravery during the battle. He also learned harsh lessons about dealing with revolutionaries. He learned how to move an army from northern Mexico into

Texas. This lesson would come in handy nearly twenty-three years later as he advanced to San Antonio de Béxar again.

He learned that defeating a revolution required more than victory in battle. That was just the start. Anyone who surrendered would also be killed. No respect would be shown to their corpses.

He also learned that Americans could be easily defeated. The frontiersmen he encountered at Medina were undisciplined and didn't put up much of a fight. He began to regard Americans with contempt.

He'd continue to receive more experience. The rallying cries to break free from Spanish control were growing.

Unlike many monarchies, the rulers in Spain were actually more tolerant than the colonies they controlled. In Mexico priests, military men, and government officials were tried in separate courts which gave them light sentences for crimes that might have meant death for a commoner. Spain wanted to eliminate this injustice and begin judging each person by the same legal standards regardless of their place in society. Some Mexicans like Santa Anna thought this was a bad idea.

His problem with the Spanish monarchy was he didn't think Mexico should be ruled by peninsulares. Antonio wasn't opposed to a strong central government where most of the decisions were made by leaders in the capital while the rest of the population had little say in the laws or in their leaders.

Although Antonio didn't want democracy, he wanted to see power given to Mexico's citizens, the criollos. He even agreed with some of those who wanted rights for Indios, the native people who had no protection under the law.

Despite this belief, Santa Anna rigorously defended Spanish power for seven years after the savage brutality at Medina. His bravery in fighting for the monarchy allowed him to rise in rank to major by the time he reached his mid-twenties. He was a young man with dedicated soldiers prepared to follow his orders.

The orders often involved techniques he'd learned from General Arredondo. He and his men plundered villages and executed rebels. Yet these brutal methods did little to slow the rebellion. If anything it just made the rebels more motivated.

South of Mexico the revolutions grew. Several countries in Central and South America succeeded in their quest for independence, although their ability to maintain stable governments left something to

*Agustin de Iturbide did everything he could to hold onto the old way of life. When he stepped down as Emperor, Santa Anna let him escape with his life. Foolishly returning to Mexico a year later, he was shot by his former soldiers.*

be desired. The officers in the Mexican Army knew it was only a matter of time before the Spanish were defeated in their home country. Even while Antonio fought the rebels in the provinces, he admired their tenacity—no matter what the odds, they refused to give up.

Fellow officers were laying down their arms and refusing to fight. In 1820 the sailors on board a Spanish ship refused to leave a port after learning their orders were to destroy rebel vessels. Instead of punishing them, their superior officers agreed not to take part in the battle.

In March of 1821, rebel forces massed not far from Jalapa, Antonio's birthplace. It was there that Antonio Santa Anna made a crucial decision, one which would affect not only the course of the revolution but the rest of his life.

He led a raid against the rebels, who were driven from their position. A number of them were killed or captured (which usually amounted to the same thing.)

Antonio was immediately promoted to lieutenant colonel.

But Antonio knew he hadn't won. Outnumbered, the rebels should have fled, returning to the relative safety of their villages. Instead they'd circled back, hiding on the periphery of the army's camp. He realized they were waiting for reinforcements. When they arrived, the next battle would be much worse and its outcome less certain.

He realized the rebels would never give up. He could not beat them. So Antonio would join them.

Antonio López de Santa Anna left camp, trailed by his soldiers. He approached the rebels' position carefully, letting them know he wanted to surrender.

Before the sun set, Antonio was not only a rebel, he'd been promoted to full colonel. Under the leadership of his new commander, General Agustín de Iturbide, Mexico succeeded in gaining its independence by the end of the year.

"Beloved Iturbide," Antonio said, pledging his loyalty, "whom all Mexico loves, we place ourselves, our guns and our lives at your disposal, for only you can give Mexico the strong and just rule it yearns for."

Antonio's loyalty wouldn't last very long. Neither would Iturbide's rule, or even his life. ■

*Proud, dictatorial and fearless in battle, Santa Anna inspired his men no matter what the odds were.*

# TREACHERY

Antonio Santa Anna was soon promoted to general. He watched proudly as Iturbide was crowned emperor, the first royal who'd been born in Mexico. He offered him unconditional support.

Until he was humiliated by the man whom he had defended.

Early in Iturbide's rule, Antonio joined the newly crowned emperor, sitting as he always did near the man who'd commanded him. Suddenly a palace official whispered that no one sat in the presence of an emperor, not even a general.

Antonio was similarly embarrassed after he tried to date Iturbide's unmarried sister. Doña Nicolasa wasn't very pretty, nor was she kind. In fact she was sixty years old, but he believed she would give him access to the wealth and power he'd dreamed of.

On the day he hoped to begin his courtship, he arrived at the palace and presented her with a bouquet of flowers. Unimpressed by Antonio's macho charm, she turned him down cold.

Before Iturbide had celebrated one year as emperor, the man he considered one of his most loyal subjects was plotting to overthrow him. Just as Antonio's loyalty towards Iturbide changed, so too did his support of Iturbide's form of government. As suddenly as Antonio embraced a Mexican emperor, he now embraced democracy.

So Iturbide was removed from power. In a rare show of compassion, Antonio allowed him to escape unharmed. When the former emperor tried to sneak back into Mexico in 1824, Antonio's soldiers shot him.

Meanwhile, Antonio helped set up a new form of government. Following the constitution of the United States, Mexico became an independent republic with both elected leaders and a decentralized government which allowed states from Veracruz to Texas to participate in lawmaking. Antonio backed equal rights for all Mexicans, from Indios to wealthy landowners and also for the first time agreed to eliminate separate courts for military men and priests.

Santa Anna left the capital of Mexico City for a quieter life. In 1825 he married Inés Garcia. Her best feature was her huge dowry, money which helped Antonio set up a new life. Near his birthplace of Jalapa he constructed a large plantation he named Manga de Clavo, or the "Spike of Clove." The ranch stretched for thousands of acres, much of it filled with cattle.

However the land was a fair distance from Veracruz, the city he was going to govern. So he also bought a nearby large estate called El Encero which was worth millions of pesos. Antonio began to enjoy the good life of a gentleman farmer and government official.

It didn't last.

Just four years after he'd helped draft the landmark 1824 Constitution, rumors grew that Antonio was plotting against the government. Officials in Mexico City demanded that he appear before them and explain his actions. Whether or not he was guilty of plotting to overthrow them, Antonio refused to answer to anyone. Instead of obeying their orders, he gathered a group of citizens from Veracruz who were loyal to him and prepared to repel the government's attack. He and his men took possession of the castle of Perote and fought off the soldiers.

The government sent more and more troops but the men were unprepared for the heat, the humidity, the sickness of the area. In her 1847 book, *Mexico and Her Military Chieftains*, Fay Robinson described the conflict. "The soldiers of Santa Anna were all from the tierra caliente [the hot and humid southern region]; men whose bodies the

*A clever disguise and perfect timing helped Santa Anna and his men emerge victorious from a battle centered here, at the Church of Santo Domingo in Oaxaca, Mexico.*

color of bronze seemed to suffer from exposure no more than metal does. The vomito [illness] had no effect on them, while the forces of the government from the tierra templada [the cooler northern areas] died by the hundreds… Santa Anna laughed at pursuit by enemies who died by the wayside from fatigue."

Santa Anna eventually was forced to retreat and led his men to the Church of Santo Domingo in Oaxaca. Taking shelter there meant the protection of the building's high, impenetrable walls, enormous locked gate and the sanctuary of the Catholic church. No opposing forces would break down the doors or storm the walls, for that would be considered sinful.

Although the walls prevented soldiers from entering, there were no rules against firing shots over the walls. The shots from the soldiers came fast and furious but for the most part they sailed well clear of their targets. On the other hand, Antonio's men, taking shelter along

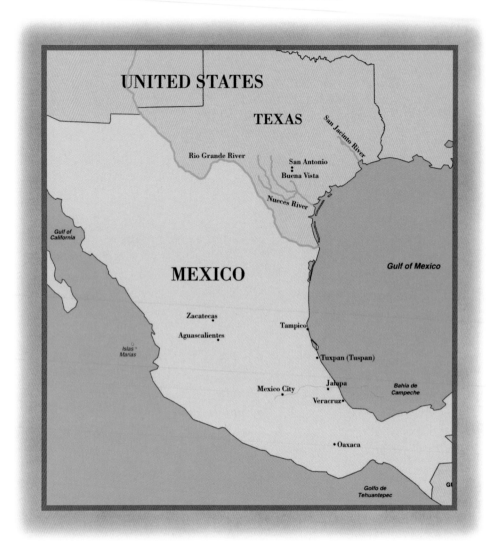

*This map shows Jalapa, Santa Anna's birthplace, as well as other Mexican and American cities where he lived, traveled, or fought battles.*

the ramparts of the high walls, were able to fire down upon their enemies.

Still Antonio realized he was outnumbered. He and his men couldn't hold the building forever. He had his men bring a large herd of oxen into the open courtyard of the church. There they saddled their horses. Driving the cattle around them, the men rushed through the doors of the church. Surprised by the animals, the Mexican Army didn't realize that Santa Anna and his men were getting away in the dust and confusion!

They didn't travel far. They rushed into another nearby church, and took their position.

The next day, according to Robinson, one officer proclaimed, "Instead of those agile soldiers so busy shooting us for three days past, I see monks in the towers. The long beards can not have joined Santa Anna!"

The officer sent most of his soldiers toward the convent Antonio had abandoned. They were between the two churches when they looked up in horror as the "monks" dropped their robes, revealing the crisp uniforms of professional soldiers. It was a trap. Antonio's men had commandeered both churches. Caught between the two points, the Mexican Army soldiers quickly surrendered.

It was good thing. By then Antonio had run out of supplies and money. He couldn't have held out much longer. He was lucky in another area as well. There really had been another revolution in Mexico. The new government welcomed Santa Anna back, and he was allowed to take over the governing of the entire state of Veracruz, instead of just the city. He also earned a seat in the new president's cabinet as Minister of War.

This time the Mexican government's timing was as good as Antonio's had been. Just when they needed the general, he was on their side.

Spain had launched an attack.■

*Looking as regal as a king, Santa Anna hired artists to paint numerous portraits of him. He always made sure he looked his best in these illustrations.*

# WAR!

## CHAPTER 5

Since Mexico's independence from Spain, an uneasy peace had existed between the two countries. Like most of Spain's former colonies, Mexico's political turmoil left it vulnerable to attack. Spain's King Ferdinand VII hoped to take advantage of that weakness.

In mid-summer, 1829, a flotilla with thousands of Spanish soldiers sailed from Cuba and landed at Tampico. According to Antonio, he was in Mexico City when news of the invasion reached him. He quickly assembled a force of 700 well-trained soldiers. He realized he'd be badly outnumbered, but once again his plans depended less on the quantity of soldiers he commanded than on the cunning of his plans.

Loading his small army in open boats, he managed to make a seventy-mile open-water passage to the port city Tuspan (modern-day Tuxpan). In Tuspan, he and his men commandeered a number of canoes and paddled across a lagoon to Tampico. When they arrived, the Spanish invaders were just a few miles away.

By the time Antonio and his men set up camp, most of the Spanish troops were headed into Mexico's interior. A thousand remained behind, but they weren't expecting trouble.

Trouble is what they got.

*The man who inspired Santa Anna—Napoleon Bonaparte. Santa Anna greatly admired the French military leader, often standing as he did and combing his hair in a similar fashion.*

At dawn on the first day of August Antonio led the attack. The battle was brief and bloody. In just four hours Antonio owned another victory. The celebration was brief, interrupted by the return of the rest of the Spanish soldiers. Antonio was heavily outnumbered and his retreat was blocked. There didn't seem to be any way out.

This time his confidence won the day. He told the Spanish General Barradas that there were thousands of Mexicans waiting nearby. If he wasn't allowed to return to his camp, he would order them to attack.

At that moment, Antonio was bluffing. By the time Barradas realized he'd been deceived, Antonio had received reinforcements. The warfare lasted just over a month. By September 11, Barradas was ready to give up. He'd lost nearly half his men, while the rest were exhausted or injured. His defeated army sailed back to Cuba.

Most historians today doubt that version of events. The invading Spanish landed at the worst possible place and worst possible time. It was the height of the yellow fever season.

So they believe that Antonio led an army north and took control of the heights overlooking Tampico. The climate was much healthier there, and his commanding position kept the Spanish bottled up in the city. Antonio waited a month while disease slowly thinned the Spanish ranks. Then he attacked. The Spanish quickly surrendered.

But everyone agrees about two things. The Spanish would never threaten their former colony again. And as the "Victor of Tampico," Antonio quickly became a national hero.

This was about the time that Antonio began calling himself the "Napoleon of the West." He even brushed his hair from back to front in imitation of his hero.

Although Mexico would suffer through revolutions for the next four years, by 1833 Antonio had gained enough popular support to be elected president. Unfortunately, as a former military commander he was uncomfortable with the give and take of a democracy. He hated to compromise. Every time he faced opposition, Antonio retreated to his ranch and his family. Each time his supporters would beg for his return. He'd accept with renewed confidence and power. Instead of compromising, Antonio got his way by acting like a grade school kid threatening to take his bat and ball if he can't play first base.

Including the times he quit and took the job back during the next twenty years, Antonio became Mexico's president eleven times. This

*This illustration shows a Santa Anna presidential inauguration. He enjoyed more of these than most presidents—he was president eleven times!*

was partly a reflection of the instability of Mexican governments. Between April 1829 and December 1844 there were twenty different presidential administrations. Thirteen other men besides Antonio would call themselves "El Presidente" during this turbulent time.

Antonio's inability to fit into the way democracies are run would not just change his political career. It would affect the lives of numerous Mexican citizens, including those living in the area which would become Texas.

The reforms of the 1824 constitution had faded in the latter part of the decade. Antonio's election to the presidency brought them back.

Once he was in office he changed his mind. "I am a conservative," he said in his autobiography, "and I offer the nation a clear program which will save it. We must have a strong central government… The Catholic Church must rule supreme. And the ancient privileges which priests and army officers enjoyed must be restored."

If the president of another democracy had made such a pronouncement, the voters would have driven him from office. But Mexicans, weary from a decade of political turmoil, generally supported the new proclamations.

Those who opposed him were savagely silenced.

The city-state of Zacatecas in central Mexico refused to relinquish democratic ideals. In early 1835, the Zacatecasans assembled a force of 13,000 men, guarded by cannons and prepared to defend the 1824 constitution. Because the area was dotted with silver mines, Antonio wasn't about to lose such an important part of the national treasury.

Unfortunately the Mexican Army was in its usual state of disarray. Even as a powerful president, Antonio could only put together 3,500 soldiers. But they were better trained and more disciplined than the rebels. Just as important, as usual Antonio had a plan.

He organized the men at Aguascalientes, about 50 miles south of the rebel forces. Then they marched north through jungle and wilderness. On the night of May 10 they reached the less protected rear area of the city of Zacatecas. When the sun rose, the order to attack came. Rebel officers fled, leaving their troops uncommanded. The slaughter was brutal, even compared to previous battles. After driving the rebel forces from the battlefield, Antonio's men swept into the unprotected city. They attacked civilians, including women and unarmed men. According to estimates, more than 2,500 people were killed in a single day of fighting.

The victory was swift. The way Antonio achieved it sent a clear message across the country he now controlled with an iron grip. He was in charge. Any opposition would be dealt with fiercely.

In Texas a small band of rebels was already organizing. They were former citizens of a country where democracy wasn't abandoned for one man's fear of compromise, or altered because of a single person's insecurity. These men would lead a revolt which would leave the map of Mexico forever altered.■

*Santa Anna met with his match against the military leadership of Sam Houston. The governor of both Texas and Tennessee, he commanded the forces which handed Santa Anna his greatest defeat.*

# THE COUNTRY OF TEXAS

## CHAPTER 6

T o United States citizens dreaming of adventure, the wild lands of Texas looked especially attractive. To settle the sparsely settled region, Mexico had originally offered individual families nearly 5,000 acres and no taxation for 10 years. The program was put in the hands of contractors called empresarios, who received huge estates in return for their recruiting efforts.

It didn't take long for word to get out. Many empty cabins along the American frontier states had the letters "G.T.T." (Gone to Texas) scrawled on their doors. By 1835, a decade after the program began, the newcomers outnumbered Mexicans in the region.

Unfortunately the new arrivals brought their share of problems, especially a desire for slaves. Slavery was illegal in Mexico.

The same political disarray which had encouraged the Spanish invasion also motivated the Texicans—as the U.S. citizens in Texas called themselves—to revolt. After all, if Mexico couldn't maintain a democracy, why should they follow the country's laws, pay taxes or give up their slaves? Although Antonio's brutal suppression of the Zacatecas uprising might have scared most Mexicans, the Texicans were sons of the American revolution. Their fathers had already produced an enduring democracy.

Most Mexicans took a less positive view of the rebels in Texas. They saw these immigrants from the United States as barbaric, like wild animals on the frontier. When they revolted, Antonio sent General Martín Cós, his wife's brother, to tame them.

Operating under an order that all U.S. citizens who'd moved to Texas since 1830 had to leave, General Cós marched into San Antonio de Béxar. There he was quickly defeated by the Texicans.

They could have killed him. They didn't. Instead they got him to promise that the Mexican Army would leave the state. Then they let him go.

His brother-in-law was not about to be bound by some pledge made under duress. Enraged by the arrogant demands of the "Yankees," he commanded an army of well-trained officers and poorly prepared conscripts. They left Saltillo in northern Mexico on January 25, 1836 and traveled beneath a red flag which meant "give no quarter." Kill them all.

By the time they reached the Alamo in February, the Texicans were ready to accept those terms.

William Travis, the fort's commander, wrote down his thoughts. These would later be found among the wreckage: "Our flag still floats proudly from the walls. We shall never surrender or retreat. Liberty or death!"

The Alamo led to both—the deaths of the Texicans eventually gave liberty to Texas.

On March 2, 1836, led by former U. S. congressman Sam Houston, the citizens of Texas declared their independence.

Despite the citizens' brave intentions, conditions quickly got worse. Within a few days of the fall of the Alamo, word of the defeat got out. Coupled with the continuing advance of Santa Anna's army, the news terrified many Texans. They hurriedly grabbed their children and a few belongings and headed east—as far from Santa Anna as they could get.

At the presidio of Goliad, not far from the Alamo, James Fannin commanded four hundred men. Fannin had quickly learned of the Alamo disaster, but waited too long to try to escape. His men were trapped in open country on March 19. After an exchange of gunfire and learning that the Mexicans had been reinforced, Fannin surrendered the following morning.

A week later, his soldiers were divided into four groups and the helpless men were gunned down in cold blood. Fewer than 30 escaped.

"Remember Goliad" now joined "Remember the Alamo" as a battle cry. But for nearly a month, the only memory that the last remaining Texan army had was of staying away from the Mexicans. Houston, their commander, was criticized for avoiding a fight.

Then on the morning of April 20, Houston took advantage of the sort of good fortune that Antonio was famous for. He received word

*Bowed and humbled, Santa Anna joins General Martín Cós in surrendering to Sam Houston following the Battle of San Jacinto.*

that Santa Anna, leading nearly 1000 troops, was heading for a ferry crossing on the nearby San Jacinto River. Houston urged his men forward. They arrived well ahead of Santa Anna, set up defensive positions and enjoyed a good meal while they rested. The Mexicans arrived later in the afternoon. They immediately began setting up defensive positions.

The next morning, Santa Anna received reinforcements. That gave him about 1,200 men to Houston's 900. Even though they were out-numbered, the Texans desperately wanted to fight. But Houston hesitated. Soon it was late afternoon. Most of Santa Anna's men had been up all night digging trenches and putting up log barriers, then on the alert since the sun had come up. They were tired.

Santa Anna made his decision. His men could stand down. He even pulled back his sentries. The general didn't believe the Texicans would attack a superior army with darkness coming on. Then he went into his tent.

"Mañana (tomorrow)," he may have thought before falling asleep. "Mañana we attack."

But there would be no "mañana" for Antonio López de Santa Anna.

Houston seized his opportunity. His men plunged into the Mexi-can camp. The outcome was decided before Antonio could put on his pants. Angry Texans shot and stabbed dazed soldiers who staggered from their tents. Many screamed "Me no Alamo—Me no Goliad." It didn't do them any good. When the killing finally stopped, more than 600 Mexicans were dead. Several hundred more were wounded. Only nine Texans died.

Houston kept his men from killing everyone and allowed a peace-ful surrender. In the confusion Antonio managed to escape. He was found the next day by a search party, standing alone and confused in a deserted prairie. He denied that he was Santa Anna and his captors believed him—until shouts of "El Presidente" greeted his arrival into the camp.

Brought before Houston, who was nursing an injury suffered in battle, Antonio declared, "Mi General, ha derrotado el Napoleon de oste!" ("You have defeated the Napoleon of the West!").

Houston was unimpressed. Aware that there were thousands of Mexican soldiers massing nearby, he forced Antonio to sign a peace treaty. While the other officers believed Antonio should be shot, he was held captive for several months. Then he traveled to Washington as a kind of ambassador between the new country of Texas and Mexico.

Houston went on to become the first president of the country of Texas. It would join the United States in 1845.

Long before that happened, Santa Anna had returned to Mexico. He had lost Texas. Soon he would lose much more.■

*Trying to pass as a common soldier after he was captured, Santa Anna was discovered when his men called out, "El Presidente!" Here he appears before an injured Sam Houston.*

*In the Battle of Buena Vista, General Santa Anna commanded 20,000 soldiers but he lost to 5,000 U.S. forces who were better equipped and better trained. The battle ended the Mexican-American war and gave the U.S. western territory along with Texas.*

# INTO EXILE
# AND INTO HISTORY

Soon after reassuming the presidency, Antonio had another crisis to deal with. Mexico had long disputed the amount of money it owed France. In 1838, a French pastry chef who owned a restaurant near Mexico City claimed that his business was wrecked by drunk and rowdy Mexican officers. He presented a bill for 800 pesos to the Mexican government. They refused to pay. When he took the debt to his own country, France added about 600,000 pesos to it. They used it as an excuse to start a conflict which became known as the "Pastry War."

French ships in Veracruz harbor fired cannonballs into the city. Antonio was there at the time and mounted a white horse. Like a knight riding to the rescue, he galloped towards the battle. An eight-pound French cannonball slammed into his left leg. It had to be amputated just below the knee. Mexico was similarly injured, being forced to borrow money from another country to pay its debt to France and end the war.

If the Pastry War was one of the oddest conflicts in history, Antonio provided one of the strangest excuses for a parade. In 1842, he persuaded a trusted aide to come to his ranch and dig up his severed leg. After all, Antonio explained, it had given its "life" for Mexico. Why shouldn't it be properly honored?

Thousands of citizens lined the streets of Mexico City. Priests and officers, peasants and landowners all crowded around, watching the military procession led by Antonio Santa Anna. A coffin containing his leg was on a wagon that followed closely behind. At the Santa Paula cemetery, the leg was buried and a monument erected in its honor.

Antonio's glory was short-lived.

1844 brought sadness to Antonio's life as his wife, Inés died. He didn't grieve for long. Just two months later the fifty-year-old Antonio married fifteen-year-old Maria Dolores de Tostar. Though the wedding was scandalous, many of Antonio's friends changed their minds when they met his wife. Maria was something of an independent woman for the time, quick-witted and unwilling to play the submissive wife role. Indeed she could often be seen dancing in Mexico City. Despite predictions of divorce, she stayed by Antonio's side for the rest of his life.

It was a life which would be marred by turmoil. The year after his marriage, Mexicans who were angered at the way Antonio was running the country revolted. They dug up his leg bone, dragged it through the street and drove him from power. He was exiled to Cuba. It was the first of his six "exiles for life."

Before he left, Antonio was able to address Congress, saying, "Napoleon, after having outraged all Europe, was exiled to St. Helena, and France, over whom he had long tyrannized, thought herself sufficiently avenged. My services have not equaled his, but I have the advantage over him in other respects. I can show by my mutilated body, that I have suffered for Mexico. The august chambers will then accept my solemn abdication of the presidency and permit me to assume eternal exile."

The exile didn't last long. When Texas voted to join the United States in 1845, an immediate dispute over the border developed. Mexico claimed all of the land below the Nueces River. The United States said it was further south, all the way to the Rio Grande River. At its widest point, the difference was more than one hundred miles.

It would take a war to settle the issue.

The country summoned Antonio back to lead it in the fight, which started in 1846 and became known as the Mexican-American War. He fought with all the cunning he could. Though a horse he was riding was shot and killed, troops under his command nearly defeated U.S. forces at Buena Vista in February of 1847. His efforts were not enough, however, as the U.S. Army was better equipped and trained. For nine months beginning in September, 1847 the U.S. flag flew over the Mexican capital.

The war ended with the Treaty of Guadalupe Hidalgo, which gave the U.S. a huge part of what had been Mexican territory. In addition to Texas, it included the future states of Arizona, California, Nevada, New Mexico and Utah in addition to portions of Colorado, Kansas and Wyoming. In exchange, the U.S. paid the Mexican government 15,000,000 dollars. In the aftermath, Antonio went into exile for five years, this time in Jamaica and Colombia.

He came back in 1853 and declared himself dictator. That lasted two years and was followed by yet another exile. Ten years later he initially supported the brief and bizarre reign of Archduke Maximilian, an Austrian nobleman, and his wife Empress Carlota. Antonio and other Mexicans decided they needed European royals to again run the country. Not surprisingly, he soon turned against Maximilian and tried to raise funds to lead an army that would overthrow the new emperor. By that time, no one took him seriously. He wasn't part of the uprising that overthrew Maximilian in 1867. The young emperor faced a firing squad and his widow returned to Europe.

Antonio spent most of his remaining years in exile, still trying desperately to regain the power and prestige he'd once enjoyed. He finally returned to Mexico in 1874 under the terms of a general amnesty. His young wife stayed with him even though they lived in poverty.

He died on July 21, 1876.

He fought more battles than his heroes Napoleon and Washington combined. His choices cost Mexico half her territory, more than one million square miles.

An obituary published on the occasion of his death perhaps said it best: "However he may have been condemned by parties, his career formed a brilliant and important portion of the History of Mexico and future historians will differ in their judgment of his merits. General Santa Anna outlived his usefulness and ambition, and died at the ripe age of eighty-two. Peace to his ashes." ■

# CHRONOLOGY

| 1794 | Born on February 21 in Jalapa |
| 1808 | Begins apprenticeship as merchant after quitting school |
| 1810 | Enlists as officer in Mexican army |
| 1813 | Fights at the Battle of Medina |
| 1821 | Switches allegiance and joins rebel forces |
| 1824 | Helps set up republican government |
| 1825 | Marries Inés Garcia |
| 1827 | Moves to his ranch Mango de Clava |
| 1829 | Defeats Spanish forces at Battle of Tampico |
| 1833 | Elected president for the first time |
| 1835 | Wins Battle of Zacetecas |
| 1836 | Defeats Texan forces at the Alamo but is soon captured at San Jacinto, which allows Texas to become an independent country; travels to Washington after his release |
| 1838 | Loses leg to a cannonball during "Pastry War" against the French |
| 1842 | Buries his leg in a well-attended religious ceremony |
| 1844 | After first wife Inés dies, marries fifteen-year-old Maria Dolores de Tostar two months later |
| 1845 | Exiled to Cuba |
| 1846 | Returns after United States declares war on Mexico |
| 1848 | Exiled to Jamaica |
| 1853 | Declares himself dictator |
| 1855 | Exiled to Colombia |
| 1859 | Exiled to the Virgin Islands |
| 1864 | Declares himself in support of Emperor Maximilian, but soon turns against him |
| 1867 | Exiled to Nassau in Bahama Islands |
| 1874 | Returns to Mexico |
| 1876 | Dies on June 21 |

# TIMELINE IN HISTORY

1521    Hernan Cortés defeats Aztecs and claims Mexico for Spain

1769    Napoleon Bonaparte is born on the Mediterranean island of Corsica

1786    Birth of Davy Crockett

1792    George Vancouver explores the coasts of Oregon and Washington, producing first maps of the Northwest

1799    Death of George Washington

1803    United States nearly doubles in size following Louisiana Purchase; Lewis and Clark Expedition to map first overland route to the Northwest begins

1810    Colombia wins independence from Spain

1821    Mexico wins independence from Spain; Spanish territories in western United States fall under Mexican control; Napoleon dies in exile on South Atlantic island of St. Helena

1827    Greece wins independence from Turkey

1837    Queen Victoria of England begins 64-year reign

1839    U.S. Army officer Abner Doubleday lays out baseball diamond and plays first game of baseball

1845    Texas admitted to Union as 45th state

1846    United States declares war on Mexico

1848    United States annexes territories which will become all or part of states of Arizona, California, Colorado, Kansas, Nevada, New Mexico, Texas, Utah and Wyoming

1849    California Gold Rush begins

1859    Benito Juarez becomes first native American president of Mexico

1861    U.S. Civil War begins

1864    French nobleman Maximilian becomes French emperor

1865    Civil War ends

1867    Maximilian overthrown and executed

1872    Juarez dies

1876    Porfirio Díaz becomes Mexican dictator; except for 1880-1884, rules until 1911

# FURTHER READING

For Young Adults:

Bredeson, Carmen. *The Battle of the Alamo: The Fight for Texas Territory.* Brookfield, CT: The Millbrook Press, 1996.

Doherty, Kieran. *Explorers, Missionaries and Trappers.* Minneapolis: The Oliver Press, Inc., 2000.

Hatt, Christine. *The American West: Native Americans, Pioneers and Settlers.* New York: Peter Bedrick Books, 1998.

Lord, Walter. *A Time to Stand.* New York: Harper and Brothers, 1961.

Michener, James. *The Eagle and the Raven.* Austin, TX: State House Press, 1990.

Sorrels, Roy. *The Alamo in American History.* Springfield, NJ: Enslow Publishers, Inc., 1996.

Works Consulted:

Crawford, Ann Fears, ed. *The Eagle: The Autobiography of Santa Anna.* Austin, TX: The Pemberton Press, 1967.

Garland, Sherry. *The Shadow of the Alamo.* New York: Gulliver Books Harcourt, Inc., 2001.

Long, Jeff. *Duel of Eagles.* New York: William Morrow and Company, 1990.

Roberts, Randy and James S. Olson. *A Line in the Sand: The Alamo in Blood and Memory.* New York: The Free Press, 2001.

Robinson, Fay. *Mexico and Her Military Chieftains.* Quoted in http://www.tamu.edu/ccbn/dewitt/santaanna.htm.

# ON THE WEB

Historical Text Archive: Santa Anna
http://historicaltextarchive.com/sections.php?op=viewarticle&artid=159

Alamo de Parras
http://alamo-de-parras.welkin.org

The Handbook of Texas Online: Santa Anna
http://www.tsha.utexas.edu/handbook/online/articles/view/SS/fsa29.html

Antonio Lopez de Santa Anna
http://www.tamu.edu/ccbn/dewitt/santaanna.htm

# GLOSSARY

centralized government - system in which decisions are made in the capitol and individual states have little power

conscript (KAHN-script) - one who is forced to join the military

criollo (cree-OH-low) - person whose ancestors are Spanish but who was born in Mexico

dowry (DOW-ree) - money and/or property given by a bride's family to her husband at the time of their marriage

flotilla (flow-TILL-uh) - group of ships

garrison – military installation or the troops at a military installation

hacienda (ah-see-EN-duh) - large ranch for cattle or horses

Indios - Native Americans

mestizo (mess-TEE-zoe) - person who is mixture of native American and criollo

peso (PAY-soh) - unit of Mexican money

presidio (preh-SID-ee-oh) - fort usually located near a mission

republic - political system which features an elected leader such as a president with power held by elected representatives

# INDEX